BLUENOSERS'
BOOK OF SLANG

HOW TO TALK
NOVA SCOTIAN

Vernon Oickle

MacIntyre Purcell Publishing Inc.

MacIntyre Purcell Publishing Inc.
194 Hospital Rd.
Lunenburg, Nova Scotia
B0J 2C0
(902) 640-3350

www.macintyrepurcell.com
info@macintyrepurcell.com

Printed and bound in Canada by Friesens

Design and layout: Alex Hickey
Cover design: Denis Cunningham
Illustrations: Julie Anne Babin

ISBN: 978-1-77276-093-4

Library and Archives Canada Cataloguing in Publication

Oickle, Vernon, 1961-, author   How to talk Nova Scotian : the
Bluenoser's book of slang / Vernon Oickle.

ISBN 978-1-77276-093-4 (softcover)

        1. English language--Nova Scotia--Slang. I. Title.

PE3245.N6O43 2018   427'.9716   C2018-900607-2

MacIntyre Purcell Publishing Inc. would like to acknowledge the financial support of the Government of Canada and the Nova Scotia Department of Tourism, Culture and Heritage.

WARNING:
This book contains words and phrases
that may be offensive.

Reader discretion advised.

This book is dedicated to my fellow Bluenosers;
those who know how to turn a phrase.

Nova Scotianisms

Every region of the world has its own distinct linguistic shorthand. They are words and expressions, nurtured and given meaning over time, that inform who we are and provide us with a common thread that — whether we know it or not — binds us together.

Nova Scotia is blessed with a rich language. It is littered with words and expressions that vary from county to county, and from fishing community to farm town. If you are really lucky, you may be left scratching your head and wondering what you've just heard. Sometimes the words are so delightfully twisted, the word or phrase turned on its ear, that it may be baffling . . . even to lexicographers.

Language, of course, derives from many sources. For example, did you know that some of the modern expressions that we use today were actually born in the fertile mind of writer and judge, Thomas Chandler Haliburton (1796-1865), whose abilities as a writer were said to have inspired Mark Twain?

Some of the verbal gems we use today came from Haliburton's books. (There is little question that Haliburton was inspired by ordinary folks in Nova Scotia and may have even pilfered some of their phrases and made them his own.) It was Haliburton who coined such phrases as: it's raining cats and dogs; honesty is the best policy; the early bird catches the worm; an ounce of prevention is worth a pound of cure; jack of all trades and master of none.

Nova Scotians are also quite capable of butchering the English language. Who else could take words like "some" and "nice" and use them as adjectives and adverbs? We proudly do that. For example, you can say, "That's a right nice vessel," or "That's some nice vessel," or "That's some vessel," but you can't say, "That's a right vessel."

This book is a collection of Nova Scotianisms. We hope it helps you understand what your neighbour may have just said — or that it provides you with a good chuckle.

— Vernon Oickle

~A~

A bag of nerves — Very nervous.

Able sailor — Strong and having a lot of stamina.

About as much fun as a heart attack — Not fun; unpleasant.

A day late and a dollar short — Come up short.

A dog's breakfast — A real mess.

A face only a mother could love — Ugly.

A face that would stop an eight-day clock — Unattractive.

A feed — A large meal.

A few bricks short of a load — Not bright; unintelligent.

Variations:
A few rooms short of a full house.
A few cards short of a full deck.
A few pennies short of a dollar.
A few cookies short of a dozen.
A few eggs short of a dozen.
A few ounces short of a pound.
A few inches short of a foot.
A few roses short of a bush.

A flat — Flat tire or 24 cans of beer.

After a little — Later on.

After grass — A second crop of grass to be made into hay on the same field in the same summer.

A goose walked over my grave! — Said when a person gets a sudden chill or shiver.

A hard-looking ticket — Disheveled and unkempt.

Ain't that somethin' — Wow, that's really something!

Ain't you a pip — A snob.

A large day — A warm, sunny day.

A little shot will do you good — A drink of liquor will help.

All but all — Almost gone.

All decked out (or all dolled up) — Dressed up and looking sharp.

Also heard as:
All dolled up and nowhere to go.

All foolish for it — Very excited.

All my born days — Expression of incredulousness.

All sunshine and roses right now — Things are seemingly going well but are expected to take a turn for the worse.

Antis — Nova Scotians who were opposed to Confederation.

Any port in a storm — Anything (or anyone) will do.

A pretty kettle of fish — A mess.

Variation:
A fine kettle of fish.

A real shit show — A real mess.

Are you coming with? — Are you coming along with me?

Are you off your rocker? — Have you lost your mind?

Arse over kettle — Slipped and fell.

Variation:
Arse over teakettle.

Article — Strange or odd person.

As goes Monday, so goes the rest of the week — An old saying predicting how your week is going to unfold especially when it seems like you are having a run of bad luck.

As pigheaded as a tractor off course — Stubborn.

As quick as a bunny — Happen very quickly.

As scarce as hen's teeth — Rare or unusual, very scarce.

A shit kicking — A hard or difficult time.

Ass is sucking wind — Used as an insult when someone is saying something that seems too good to be true.

As slow as cold molasses going up a hill in the middle of January — Very slow.

As sure as Christ made little apples — Definite.

Ass wipe — A nasty or insincere person; someone who lies or brags.

A whuppin' — A beating.

Back-ass-wards — Ass backwards.

Backed up — Constipated or having more work to do than you can possibly get done.

Bad things happen in threes — A prophecy of bad news, predicting more bad news will follow.

Baffle them with bullshit — Fool them.

Baiting deer — Setting out apples to attract deer for hunting purposes.

Balls against the wall — Up against difficulty.

Banged up — Injured.

Banker — A fishing schooner typically used on the Grand Banks.

Basket case — Hysterical or distraught person.

Batten down the hatches — Hatches on a ship, or a caution to prepare for bad weather.

Beat the feet — Hurry up; get moving.

Beans — Traditional Saturday night meal, which always includes baked beans.

Bed-lunch — Snack before going to bed at night.

Bed lunch

Been around since dirt was rocks — Old.

Bestkind — A good thing.

Better than a kick in the arse with a frozen boot — Could have been worse.

> *Variations:*
> Better than a kick in the teeth.
> Better than a sharp stick in the eye.

Between hay and grass — The time in late winter or early spring when the barn loft is empty and there is no hay in the fields.

Biff — Throw something.

Big blow — Very strong and powerful winds.

Big feeling — Arrogant or self-important.

Big rough on — A stormy sea.

Big snow, little snow or little snow, big snow — Big snowflakes mean little accumulation and vice-versa.

Bite it off and spit it out — Tell the truth.

Blabber mouth — Someone who can't keep a secret.

Blat — Cry or whine.

Bloaters — Herring that has been salted.

Block — An area of an apple orchard.

Blow a gasket — Get angry.

Variation:
Blow a fuse.

Blowin' a gale — Very windy.

Blowing smoke up your arse — Furtively flattering.

Blueberry grunt — A regional recipe using stewed blueberries and dumplings.

Variation:
Blueberry buckle.

Blueberrying — Picking blueberries.

Bluenoser — A Nova Scotian.

Boiling — Very angry or upset.

Boil-up — A cup of tea and a snack enjoyed during a quick break from hard work or a rough sea.

Book learnin' — Education.

Bootlicker — Someone who sucks up to the boss or person in a position of authority.

Bootin' 'er — In a rush or hurry.

Bone up — Pay back a debt.

Bored or punched — Discontented.

You can't tell that girl anything because she's got so much book learnin'

Boston States — New England, a region with which Nova Scotians have had extremely close ties.

Bottom feeder — Low life.

Boughten bread — Bread purchased at a store, as opposed to homemade bread, usually sliced.

Brake burn — A mark left on a road after a car brakes hard and skids – brake burns are often made deliberately and competitively on rural roads.

Bread poultice — A homemade remedy using bread, hot water, salt water and butter (or shortening.) Used to draw infection out of a cut or other bodily ailment.

Breaking wind — Farting.

Breezin' up — Windy.

Bright as a burned-out light bulb — Stupid, unintelligent.

Browned off — Very mad.

Brownnoser — Someone who sucks up to the boss or person in a position of authority.

Buckle down — Get down to work; pay attention.

Bud — A friend or pal; or used when you don't remember somebody's name.

Buddy — A generic name for "that fellah," or any person whose name one does not know.

Bug eyed — Surprised or curious.

Bug off — Leave me alone.

Built like a dory plug — Short and plump.

Variation:
Built like a brick shithouse.

Bum-by — Get around to it later.

Bummed — Disgusted or fed up.

Burning season — That traditional time in early spring when Nova Scotians burn grass and bushes around their property.

Burnt your ass — Made angry.

Bust a gut — Have a good laugh.

Butcher — Destroy something.

Butt ugly — Very ugly.

Buzz off — Go away.

By and by — Sooner or later.

By the thundering — An exclamation of surprise.

Variations:

By the Lord thundering Jesus.

By the Lord rattling Jesus.

Calv'd — Delivered a calf.

Came in on the fog — Came in from a place unknown.

Can't do squat — Unable to do much.

Can't get blood from a turnip — Can't get money from someone who doesn't have money.

> *Variations:*
> Can't get blood from a stone.
> Can't squeeze blood from a turnip/stone.

Can't get out of his/her own way — Someone who is basically clumsy or self-absorbed.

Can't saddle horses — Can't make people get along.

Can't see for looking — Can't see whatever you are looking for.

Can't shine shit — Unable to make things look better than they are.

Can't win for losing — Having a string of bad luck.

Cape Islander — Someone from Cape Sable Island. Also, a small wooden boat.

Caper — Someone from Cape Breton.

Card party — A gathering at home or in a community hall where people get together to play cards, often competitively and often for money or prizes.

Case of drop-ass — Tired or lazy.

Cat's meow — Special or superior.

Variation:
Cat's ass.

Cat's jump — Short distance.

Ceilidh — (Pronounced kay-lee.) Common term on Cape Breton Island, meaning informal social gatherings featuring Scottish/Irish dancing, music and story telling.

Cellar porch — A structure over the outside entrance to a house cellar.

CFA (Come From Away) — Someone who has moved to Nova Scotia from elsewhere.

Chesterfield — Couch.

Chewier than a boiled owl — Very tough and dry to eat.

Chewing the fat — Having a casual conversation.

Chew nails and spit tacks — Very nasty.

Chimley — Chimney.

Chin wag — A conversation.

Chow-chow — Preserve made from green tomatoes, sugar and spices and cooked over the stove.

Chow down — Eat.

Clambake — A social function involving freshly dug clams, boiled in saltwater and served right on the beach. It can also be in reference to sex on the beach.

Clammer — A person who digs clams.

Clap your trap — Shut up and stop talking.

Clear as mud — Very confusing.

Clipping right along — Moving at a fast and steady pace.

Clodhoppers — Large feet.

Clogged up — Constipated.

Close cousins — Cousins who grew up either in the same house, or very close by. Close cousins know each other almost like siblings and feel like close family – whether they are first, second, third cousins or even more distantly related.

Clodhoppers

Cold enough to freeze the balls off a brass monkey — Very, very, very cold.

Variation:
Cold as a witch's teat.

Come aboard'er — Put some muscle behind it.

Come on to it — Try harder; use more force.

Comin' with? — Are you coming with me?

Community/Church breakfast/tea/supper/ — A meal prepared by a community organization and served in a community or church hall, used as a fundraiser. Communities strive to become known for having the best of a certain kind of supper, breakfast or tea.

Examples:

Strawberry Shortcake Supper (a meal with strawberry shortcake for dessert.)

Blueberry Supper (a meal followed by various blueberry desserts.)

Variety Supper (a little bit of everything; like a potluck, but you don't have to bring anything except money to pay for your supper.)

Ham and Scalloped Potato Supper.

Turkey Supper.

Chowder Supper.

Scallop Supper.

Lobster Supper.

Waffle Breakfast.

Pancake Breakfast.

Traditional Breakfast (usually eggs, bacon, sausage, beans, toast and home fries, tea, coffee and/or juice.)

Christmas Tea (usually held in the afternoon with tea, coffee, sandwiches and a wide assortment of sweets.)

Ice Cream Sundae Social (another afternoon affair featuring ice cream with all the toppings.)

Cooking up a batch — Making a recipe.

Cooking with gas — Getting things done in an efficient manner.

> *Variation:*
> Pumping with gas.

Could stretch a mile but I'd have to walk back — Tired or lazy.

Counting crows — Being superstitious.

Cracked in the head — Not in the right frame of mind.

Cracking on — Leave.

Cracklin' — Salt fish cooked with salt pork scraps.

Crack upside the head — Hit or gesture to hit you aside the head.

Crank-ass — Ornery person.

> *Variation:*
> Crank-pot.

Crazier than a bag of loons — Very crazy, loony.

Crazier than crazy — Extremely crazy.

Crazy as a bag of hammers — Very fun loving.

Croaked — Died.

Crooked as a stovepipe — Dishonest.

Cross-grained — Very hateful, mean or angry.

Crow about it — Brag.

Cruisin' for a bruisin' — Picking a fight.

Crusty — Old and cranky.

Cuff — Strike.

Cunning — Cute or pretty.

Curtain twitchers — People who stay inside mostly, but keep close tabs on their neighbours.

Cut, split and delivered — Firewood delivered already cut up.

~D~

Dal — Short for Dalhousie University.

Damaged goods — Someone facing lots of problems or carrying lots of emotional issues.

Dead as a doornail (or doorknob) — No life left.

Dead soldier — Empty liquor bottle.

Deadwood — Something no longer useful or productive, especially when used to refer to a person.

Dearee — Term of endearment but sometimes used condescendingly.

Depends upon how you hold your mouth — When you want things to go a certain way, a lot depends on your attitude.

De-thaw — Take frozen food out of the freezer.

Devil dogs — A type of dessert; two small chocolate cakes held together with white icing.

Devil's darning needle — Dragonfly.

Didillysquat — Of no value; nothing.

Digby chicks — Salt herring snacks.

Ding-dong dash — A child's game in which children knock on a door (or ring a doorbell) and then run away before someone answers.

Dingle — Telephone call, or a historical tower in Halifax built in 1908.

Dinky car — Die-cast cars that kids play with.

Dinner — Lunch, noon meal.

Dinner pail — Lunch box.

Dirt jockey — Farmer.

Dirty — Description of bad weather.

Dit-wit — Mentally slow person.

Divvy up — Divide.

Do dirt — Explore sexual arousal.

Doeskin — Popular plaid jacket.

Doesn't know his or her arse from a hole in the ground — Very confused or bewildered.

Doesn't know if he is bored, punched or chewed by a rat — Confused.

Do fish swim in the ocean? — Sarcastic response to someone who is asking the obvious.

Variation:
Do hens lay eggs?

Do-flickey — Something you don't know the name for but you know how it is used.

Variations:
Do-hickey.
Do-jiggy.

Doing the trail — Driving around the Cabot Trail.

Donair

Donair — A sandwich wrapped in pita bread that features spicy meat, tomatoes, onions and a distinctly Nova Scotian sauce which is sweet, creamy and garlicky.

Done like yesterday's dinner — Completed a task, come to the end of the line, or can't continue doing whatever it is you're doing.

Done me the dirt — a person who has wronged another person; often by stealth or spreading rumours.

Done out — To clean out a room or a house. Very tired.

Don't be a shit-arse — Don't be a fool; don't do anything crazy.

Don't be so foolish! — Be serious.

Don't be so ignorant! — Don't act disrespectful or foolish.

Don't blow a fuse — Just calm down; take it easy.

Variation:
Don't blow a gasket.

Don't blow smoke up my arse — Don't lie to me or try to impress me.

Don't chew (bite) my head off — Don't get angry at me.

Don't dilly dally (sometimes heard as don't dilly dally Sally, regardless if it's aimed at a male or female) — Don't be slow.

Don't have a conniption — Relax; take it easy.

Variations:
Don't have a cow.
Don't have a hairy.

Don't have a pot to piss in (or a window to throw it out) — Down on your luck, financially.

Don't know diddly-squat — Uninformed.

Don't know if your ass is bored or punched — Indecisive.

Don't know shit — Not very well informed.

Variation:
Don't know squat.

Don't poke a pig — Don't continue to argue with an angry person.

Don't pussyfoot around — Stop wasting time and get to the point.

Don't strain your bacon — Don't over exert yourself.

Don't strain your brain — Don't think too hard, or when said sarcastically, don't be so stupid.

Don't take any wooden nickels — Be careful who you trust.

Don't yank my chain — Don't tell me things to make me angry.

Do the loop — Drive around town.

Dooryard — The yard outside of your house.

Dory — A small boat with a flat bottom and high sides, sharp on both ends. This boat was designed for stability.

Dough boys — A mixture of cold water and flour served in stews.

Variation:
Dough boils.

Dough funkers — Fried balls of dough; eaten with molasses and butter.

Downceller — In the basement (pronounced downCELLah.)

Down East — With the prevailing wind, the old coastal sailing route from Boston to Nova Scotia.

Down home — Going home.

Down shore — Down wind.

Down South — The United States, most often referring to the state of Florida. More recently, it has come to mean a Southern holiday.

Down Street — To go to the downtown core.

Down the hatch — Drink up.

Down the road — Go on a trip.

Draggy — Tired or run down; not feeling well.

Dress your feet — Put your shoes on.

Drier than a fart in a desert — Very hot and dry.

Drink like fish — To regularly drink a lot of alcoholic beverages.

Drive'er! — Work very hard.

Drop ass (or dragging ass) — Really tired or exhausted.

Dropped a load — Had a bowel movement.

Dropped an air biscuit — Farted.

Dropsies — Constantly dropping things.

Drove right up — Very busy.

Dry foot — A landlubber, someone who does not like going out on the water.

Duff — The dough mixture added to stew or also a word used for a type of pudding that contains molasses.

Dumb as a block of ice — Stupid.

Variations:
Dumb as a doornail.
Dumb as a doorknob.
Dumb as a stick.
Dumb as a stump.

Dull as dishwater — Someone with no personality.

Dumping day — The first day of the lobster fishing season; the day when lobster traps can be deployed.

Dutcher — A homemade biscuit made from flour, water, lard (or shortening) and salt.

Dutch mess — A dinner consisting of salt cod, potatoes and fried pork scraps.

Eat crow — Humiliated for having to admit a mistake.

Empty the applecart — Have a bowel movement.

Eyes are like two piss holes in the snow — Have red eyes or tired eyes, especially after a drinking session.

~ F ~

Face on it like a slapped ass — Very ugly.

Fagged out — Very tired.

Fair to middlin' — Not bad.

Fair to poor — Not so good.

Fallish — Autumn weather.

Far be it for me to say anything — It's not my place to give an opinion.

Fart in a mitten — Lots of energy.

Farting in a windstorm — Futile.

Feeding the gulls — Seasick.

Feed of smelts — A ritual in Nova Scotia of a feast of the fresh water fish called smelts.

Feed your appetite — Have something to eat.

Feel like dog meat — Dead tired or exhausted.

Find a penny pick it up, all day long you'll have good luck — Superstition relating to good luck.

Fine kettle of fish — A mess or trouble brewing.

Fill yer boots — Go ahead.

Fil-um — A local pronunciation of "film."

Finest kind — Top quality, good news.

Fired up — Very excited.

Firemen's breakfast — A community breakfast prepared and served at a local firehall as a fundraiser for a Volunteer Fire Department.

First-footed — First person through the door on New Year's Day.

Fishcakes — A maritime dish made with fish and potatoes or a term of endearment.

Fish Fry — A community supper serving fish and chips.

Fish or cut bait — Do the work or quit; also used to encourage somebody to make a decision.

Fitted out — To dress appropriately (for a fishing trip.)

Flat-ass calm or flat calm — Mirror glassiness on the ocean in early evening, dawn or before a storm.

Flat out crazy — Very busy.

Flat roundie — Flat tire.

Floored — Very surprised.

Floor it! — Speed up; go faster.

Flowage — A water body created by damming, usually beaver handiwork.

Flung dung — Angry.

Flying axe handles — Diarrhea.

Fly right into one — Get angry.

Fog along the coast — The last sentence in almost every Nova Scotian weather report.

Fog bank — An area of fog.

Fog in low-lying areas — Almost as common as "Fog along the coast."

Fog line — The boundary of an area that is more likely to experience frequent fog.

For cripe's sake — Expression of disgust or frustration.

Variations:
For Christ's sake.
For Shit's sake.
For Pete's sake.
For Pity sake.
For Frig sake.
For God's sake.
For Heaven's sake.

For crying out loud — Expression of disgust.

Forerunner — Warning or foreboding of death.

Fowsty — Smell very bad.

Freezin' me arse off — Feel very cold.

Frenchy's — A successful chain of stores in Nova Scotia that sells used clothing from the Boston States.

Fresh-it — Spring run-off that causes the riverbanks to over flow.

Fried (or baked or wasted) — Drunk or stoned or overtired.

Fried doughs — A Nova Scotian treat of fried bread dough usually served with molasses for dipping.

Frig it — Oh, what the hell. It doesn't matter.

Frig off — An angry retort, or words of disbelief.

From asshole to appetite — Everything.

From the frying pan to the fire — From one bad situation into a worse situation.

Fudgesticks — A substitute swear word for the F***word.

Full of piss and vinegar — Lots of enthusiasm.

Fussbudget — A person who is always complaining.

Gaff — Boathook used for various fishing tasks; a hook on a longer pole used by sealers.

Gaffer — Young, energetic person; alternatively, an older man.

Get after it — Go ahead and do it.

Get a grip — Calm down or take it easy.

Get onto it — Buckle down and get to work; get the job done.

Get the lead out — Get moving.

Getting on me nerves — Somebody who is irritating.

Get your ass in gear — Get moving.

Get your dancing boots on — Prepare to go out for a good time.

Get your poop together — Get down to business; organize yourself.

Geez Louise — Expression of disbelief.

Git — Get going.

Gitch — Underwear.

Give a gander — Take a look.

Giv'er — Go really hard or fast; work hard.

Gives me the willies — Makes one nervous; conjures up a feeling of disgust.

Glom onto — Grab hold of something; understands a concept.

Go away (with ya) — Expression of disbelief or doubt.

God luv'er — An expression of empathy or support or sorrow.

Goes right through ya — Digests quickly.

Going down the road — Literally, going down the road. Mainly refers to people who are leaving the province to find work elsewhere, traditionally in Upper Canada but more recently places like Alberta and BC.

Going flat out — Very busy.

Going gangbusters — Going very well.

Going lickity-split — Moving very quickly.

Going like a gas fed duck — Moving quickly.

Going nutsville — Going crazy.

Going out to bingo — An outing to a community bingo game.

Going out town — Driving to the nearest community that has a store or two.

Going out West — Heading to any place west of Quebec.

Going to see a man about a horse — Going to urinate.

Going up North (to work) — Going to work in Nunavut.

Going troutin' — Fishing.

Going up to Halifax — No matter where you live in Nova Scotia, you're "going up to Halifax."

Going up to the lake — Going to spend time at one's cottage beside a lake.

Good night, Effie — Expression of something traumatic.

Good night nurse — Expression of exclamation.

Go on with ya (g'wan wit ya) — Expression of disbelief along the lines of 'Get out of here; stop that; what are you talking about?'

Go outside and get the stink blown off — Go outside and play.

Go piss up a rope — Get lost.

Got a stick up your ass — In a bad mood.

Got done — Quit a job, or was let go.

Got herself pregnant — Used to describe a woman who is expecting a baby. Often used to describe a young, unmarried woman.

Got his/her ass handed to him/her — Lost very badly.

> *Variation:*
> Got his/her ass whupped.

Got his/her back-side (or ass) up — Became mad or upset.

Goulash — Popular Nova Scotian meal consisting of macaroni, fried hamburg and onions, mixed with tomato soup.

Grassin' — Having sex outside in a field.

Greasy out — Really slippery.

Growly — In a bad mood.

Grunt — Low skilled work.

Gull gaze — Daydream.

Gussied up — Dressed up.

G'wan witcha — That can't possibly be true.

Gull gazing

~H~

Half a mind — Considering something.

Half cut — Half drunk.

Half in the bag — Half drunk.

Hali — Halifax.

Haligonian — Someone from Halifax.

Hammered — Very drunk.

Hang her alongside — A sailing term meaning to dock alongside another ship or wharf.

Hankerin' — Longing for, especially food.

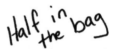

Half in the bag

Happier than a pig in shit — Very content.

Variations:
Happier than a clam at a clambake.
Happier than a rooster in a hen house.

Happy as a clam — Very happy.

Hard as nails and twice as rusty — Very tough.

Hard-assed — Very tough.

Hard lookin' ticket — Somebody who has lived a hard life.

Hardshell — A lobster that hasn't molted yet.

Haul ass — Move fast.

Hauling in — Going to storm.

Haul over the coals — Give a hard time to.

Have a feed — Eat a big meal.

Have to see a man about a horse — Have to urinate.

Head'ner — Leaving, heading out.

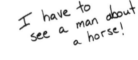

Heebie jeebies — Strange or weird feeling, usually brought on by a previous experience.

Hen party — Get together of two or more women.

Herring chokers — Fishermen; also somebody from New Brunswick.

Herring packer — Person who works in a fish processing plant.

He/she could fall into a bucket of shit and come out smellin' like a rose — Lucky person.

He/she could live off the smell of an oily rag — Very stingy.

He/she got creamed — Suffered a major defeat.

He/she has a mouth like an eight-day clock — Talks a lot.

He's so dense (or stupid) he has hair on his knuckles — Demonstrates a lack of intelligence.

Highliner — The captain of the ship that brings back the largest catch.

High tail it out of here — Go on, get moving.

Hisself — Himself.

Hitch in my step — Feeling lame.

Variation:
Hitch in my getalong.

Hit the hay — Go to bed. (Most mattresses were once filled with hay.)

Hit the sheets — Go to bed.

Hodgepodge — A traditional summertime meal consisting of new garden vegetables boiled and bathed in cream. It can also be used to describe a mess of things as in, "The crime scene was a real hodgepodge of possible clues."

Hold your pippy — Be patient.

Variation:
Hold your water.

Hold your tongue — Stop talking; resist the urge to say anything.

Holy liftin'! — Exclamation of disbelief.

Variations:
Holy F-ing Christ!
Holy Hannah!
Holy Hell!
Holy moly!
Holy Mother of God!
Holy snapping assholes!
Holy snapping mackerel!

Homely as a board fence — Unattractive.

Honest to frig — Sincerely.

Honest truth — I'm not lying.

Hoofed it — Ran very fast.

Hoot and holler — Be loud, especially at a party.

Hornier than a hop toad — To be sexually motivated.

Hot to trot — Ready to get going.

How's it (she) hanging? — How are you doing?

Variations:
How's life treatin' ya?
How's she going?

How's the feet and ears? — Greeting among friends.

Hug it out — Be friends.

Hundred-mile-an-hour tape — Red sheathing tape, especially when used to repair something on a car or truck.

Hunker down — To throw yourself into whatever you're doing; to stay put during a storm and wait the weather out.

~I~

I can't look back — Find it hard to remember.

If brains were dynamite, he wouldn't have enough to blow his nose — Demonstrating no intelligence.

Variation:
If brains were dynamite, she wouldn't
    have enough to blow her hair straight.

If brains were water his head would be a desert — Not very bright.

If I was playing for shit I wouldn't get a smell — Futile or impossible.

If you don't like the weather, wait five minutes or drive five miles — Advice expressing how changeable and how local the weather is in Nova Scotia.

If you kill one, 50 more show up to its funeral — A lot of blackflies.

I know the ins and outs of him/her — Know somebody well.

I'll box your ears — Usually an empty threat to get somebody to do a particular task.

I'm croakin' — Hot, tired, hungry, thirsty or exhausted; or desiring a cigarette.

I'm so far behind, I think I'm first — Overwhelmed.

I'm so far behind, I think I'm first!

I'm telling you straight — Telling the truth.

In a pig's ear — Expresses defiance.

Inhaled "yeah" — Yes, confirmation.

In knots — Nervous or worried.

In the pit — Work in the ground; work at a job you don't like.

Irregardless — A bastardization of the actual word "regardless."

Islander — Someone from Cape Sable Island.

It happens when it happens — Can't rush things no matter how badly you want them.

It's all gone to hell — It doesn't work anymore; nothing seems right anymore.

It's an ill wind that blows no good — A forewarning of bad fortune.

It's comin' down hard — Raining very hard.

It's flat ass out there — Not a ripple on the water.

It's like pulling teeth from a horse — Very difficult situation or task.

I've got that in me arse pocket — No sweat; I've got it covered.

I wouldn't trust you as far as I could throw you — Not trustworthy.

~ J ~

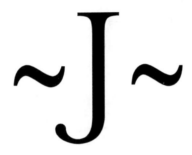

Jack — Hunt illegally at night, using a light.

Jag — Big load.

Jagged — To have consumed slightly too much liquor.

Jam, jams — Type of shortbread cookie made with jam added to an indent made with one's thumb.

Jeet? — Did you eat yet?

Jeezly — Not so good.

Jesus, Jesus, Jesus! — A forceful exclamation of surprise, excitement, dismay, anger, impatience or frustration.

Jesus, Mary and Joseph — An angry retort, allowing the user to escape the accusation of cussing, merely stating the reference to the bible.

Jesus Murphy — A variation on the above with an Irish twist.

Jigger — Use a hook on a hand line to catch fish.

Jig school — Skip school; play hooky.

Jig time — In very short order, very soon.

Jizzicked — Broken beyond repair.

Junk — Cut wood into firewood length prior to splitting.

Keep your eyes peeled — Be on the lookout; vigilant.

Keith's — A popular beer made in Nova Scotia: Alexander Keith's India Pale Ale.

Kick the can — A street game played by children.

Kick your arse up the back of your neck — Warning to someone that you will harm him or her.

Kitchen party — An informal gathering of friends and family, which inevitably ends up in the kitchen.

Knobby — Grouchy or in a bad mood.

Knocked for a loop — Caught off guard.

Knock kneed Christ — A rarely used expression of frustration.

Knock wood — Expression to maintain good luck.

Laced him/her out — Yelled at.

Lard-ass — Lazy.

Last going off — The last time.

Last off — Final point in a conversation.

Variation:
Last thing.

Last time that happened three wise men came by — Unusual occurrence.

Laughed me hole out — Laughed very hard.

Leak — To urinate.

Ledge — Bedrock.

Lernt — Learned.

Let me chew on it — I will think it over.

Let the stink blow off — Command to go outside usually aimed at children.

Lift your ass — Get moving.

Like blowing in the wind — Futile or hopeless.

Like fun — Means the opposite as in 'I don't think so.'

Like getting into a pissing contest with a skunk — Taking a lawyer to court.

Like I need a hole in the head — Don't need it at all.

Like shit to a stick — Go together very well.

Like shit to a woolen blanket — Very clingy.

Like the crack of a dog's ass — Very quickly.

Like the dickens — Give it your all.

Like the feller said — Agreement.

Like trying to catch a fart in a fishnet — Futile.

Like watchin' a kettle boil — Very slowly.

Like water through cheesecloth — Very easy.

Linter — A lean-to shed structure on the side of a building.

Lit — Pleasantly drunk.

Little Christers — A group of children, especially when they are behaving badly.

Liver and onions — A regional dish featuring fried liver and onions; sometimes also fried with bacon.

Liverpudlians — People from Liverpool.

Living gale — Bad storm at sea.

Lobstah — Lobster.

Lobstering — Lobster fishing.

Lobster roll — A mixture of lobster and mayo served on a bun, sometimes with lettuce and other ingredients like celery.

Looks good on ya — Compliment or insult.

Looks like he/she has been through the Boer War — Looking haggard and unkempt.

Lord dyin' — Exclamation of surprise or dismay.

Variations:
The Lord dyin'.
The good Lord dyin'.

Lord liftin' — Expression of exasperation.

Lord liftin'!

Lordy Lordy — Mild expression of exasperation or surprise.

Lost it — Became angry.

Lump — To remove scallops from a boat.

Lumper — Someone who removes scallops from a boat.

Lunch — Snack.

Lunenburg bump — An architectural feature found on homes in the town of Lunenburg featuring a dormer built over either the front or back door, or maybe both.

Lunenburg
Bump

Lunenburgers — People from Lunenburg.

~M~

Mackerel sky, never dry — Grey streaks in the evening sky indicate rain.

Variation:
Mackerel sky, not 24 hours dry.

Mackerel snappers — Fishermen.

Made a field — Cut grass and made hay.

'Magine — I imagine, used to express agreement with a statement someone else has just made.

Make away with it — Get rid of.

Make love to it — Obsession with it.

Make tracks — To depart.

Me ole trout — Term of endearment.

Mermaid tears — Sea glass or beach glass.

Me son — Term of affection. (Kinship not necessary, but denotes a connection of some sort.)

Mess off — Leave me alone.

Middens — Remnants of seashells or lobster or crab shells found on the beach.

Milding up outside — Getting warmer.

Mind like a sieve — Forgetful.

Mind your mouth (or tongue) — Watch what you say.

Mollywoggen — Gently rough someone up.

Moon dogs — Clouds around the moon.

Moose hole — A trap.

More frustrated than a one-arm paperhanger with an itchy butt — Very frustrated; normally to do with an extremely difficult task.

Mother — Mom, but also used by some Nova Scotians to address their wife.

Mouthpiece — Someone who talks incessantly.

Muckle onto — Grab; hug tightly.

Mud pies — Unbaked chocolate cookies made with cocoa, oatmeal and coconut.

Mud season — Mid-March to mid-April when back roads and unpaved driveways become virtual tank traps. Sometimes Nova Scotians will say they have winter, mud season, construction season and huntin' season.

Mug up — Have a beer or have a snack usually with a mug of tea.

My arse is dragging — Very tired; exhausted.

My back teeth are floating — Need to urinate very badly.

My nerves is bad — I feel anxious.

My off's all — My vacation is over.

~N~

Naked as a jaybird — Wearing a birthday suit.

NASCAD — (Pronounced nas-kad.) Nova Scotia College of Art and Design.

Neck of the woods — Certain neighbourhood or area.

Negative Nellie — A person who sees the downside of everything.

Never argue with a bulldog — An argument with somebody who is unpersuadable.

Never argue with a bulldog

New broom sweeps clean but an old one knows the corners best — Wisdom and experience count.

News bag — A gossip.

Nice as pie, simple as dishwater — Friendly but naive.

Nice day, ain't it, you? — Speaking of the weather.

Nice day for a duck — It's raining.

Nine ways to Sunday — Many ways to do something.

Nippy — Cold.

No bigger than a fart — Small.

Noggin — Glass of hot rum.

No grass under my feet — I don't waste time; I know how to get things done.

No, jue? — No, did you?

No odds — That doesn't matter.

Nor'Easter — A strong coastal storm that requires cold air meeting warm, a source of moisture and a strong jet stream.

Nort Tidney — North Sydney (primarily a Cape Breton term.)

No-see-ums — Tiny flies that you can't see but give a mighty bite.

Nosey Nelly — Very nosey.

No skin off my nose — Makes no difference; doesn't bother me.

Variations:
No skin off my arse.
No skin off my teeth.

Not a happy camper — Discontented, unhappy, upset.

Not fussy — Something doesn't have to be perfect to be useable or edible.

Not many tools in the shed — Unintelligent.

Not since Christ was a cowboy — A long time ago.

Nova Scotian Slippers — A pair of rubber boots cut off around the ankles for easy access to get to the woodpile, take out garbage, etc.

Now, mind me — Pay attention.

Numble-nuts — Slow, mentally. Someone who is clumsy; also used when you can't remember a guy's name.

Nut-bar; nut-case; nut-job — Crazy person.

Nuttier than a fruitcake — Fun-loving, crazy.

Offish — Unfriendly.

Oh, about 5'3 — Typical response when someone asks what you're up to; that is, unless you are 5'3.

Oh me nerves — Expression of anxiety or frustration, usually brought on by another person.

Oh my land — Exclamation of disbelief.

Okey dokey — Okay.

Older than dirt — Very old.

Variations:
Older than time itself.
Older than Moses himself.
Old as Methuselah.

Ole trout — Slick or sleazy person.

On a tear — In a rush or on a drinking binge.

One-eyed trouser trout — Penis.

One-holer — Outside toilet with one hole.

One-lunger — One-engine boat.

Only got one oar in the water — A little slow.

On to it — Understanding of the task at hand and getting to work on it.

Out back — Behind the house.

Out of the clear blue sky — Suddenly.

Out to lunch — Crazy.

Out South — To go across the province toward the Atlantic south from the Annapolis Valley.

Out West — Any place west of Ontario.

Over board — Go too far.

Over home — Your house; the place you grew up and to which you return with some frequency.

Owly — Cranky.

Party pans — Muffins.

Pass the bucket — Going to vomit.

Patchy fog — Lighter fog with clearer areas or breaks.

Pay for a dead horse — Pay for something used and useless.

Pecker cheque — Family allowance or child support cheque that Canadians receive from the federal government to help cover the expenses associated with child rearing.

Peddling his/her ass — Promiscuous, looking to have sex.

Peddling your legs off to give your ass a rest — Biking.

Peeling tires — Squealing tires.

PE Islander — A person from Prince Edward Island.

Petty pans — Cupcakes.

Pick — Tease.

Pig out — Eat a lot.

Pinch of salt — Personality traits that make a person interesting.

Piss across a fair wind — Try something very difficult.

Piss poor — Not good.

Piss up a rope and play with the steam — Something you might say to someone in the heat of an argument, especially if you think you're losing.

Pitter patter, let's get at 'er — Let's get going.

Plastered — Intoxicated.

Please and thank you with sugar on top — Expression of gratitude.

Pogey cheque — Government employment insurance.

Poor man's fertilizer — Late March snowstorm.

Poor man's food — A traditional name for lobster.

Pop — Soft drink.

Pothole season — That time of year, usually in the spring following the winter thaw, when the roads are in very bad shape.

Pot-licker — Suck up.

Poverty grass — Grass that grows up on a field overgrown with weeds.

Pound sand — Go away, get lost!

Pouring a living sea — Raining very hard.

Primed — Ready to go.

Pritnear — Very close, "pretty near."

Proper thing — Meets with approval.

Variation:
Good and proper.

Pumped — Excited.

Punch-drunk — In a good mood.

Punt — Small, round-bottomed boat.

Put a sock in it — Be quiet or shut your mouth.

Put the kettle on — Make tea; sometimes used as a way of saying, "We have visitors."

Put the moves on — Flirt, attempt to seduce.

Putting on — Pretending.

Putting out — Accepting a solicitation of sexual engagement.

Put to right — Make amends or to put things back to the original status.

Put your back into it — Give it all you've got.

Put your foot to the floor! — Speed up; go faster.

Quiet behind the eyes — Dull, uninterested in life.

Quiet outside — No wind; the air is very calm.

Quit pickin'! — Stop teasing me!

Quit while you're behind — Don't try anymore. Effort would be futile.

~R~

Raining like a son-o-bitch — Extreme downpour.

Ran roughshod over it — Acted without caring how it will impact others.

Rappie pie — An Acadian delicacy featuring chicken and/or pork and grated potatoes, combined in a casserole. It is sometimes served with molasses.

Rate — Right.

Rear — Back section of a community or sections of land, often deemed less desirable.

Red sky at night, sailors' delight. Red sky at morning, sailors take warning! — A red sunset foretells fair weather the following day, a red sunrise foretells stormy weather.

Ribbing — Poking fun at, teasing.

Right — Used in place of "very."

Right some good, you — Damn good; the very best.

Right out sideways — Very, very busy.

Variation:
Right out straight.

Rimracked — Destroyed.

Rip-snorter — A joke or prank that is very funny.

Rock your worries away — Rocking fast in a rocking chair.

Roundie — Tire.

'Roundtoit — Get around to it.

Rubber — Condom.

Rubbers — Rubber boots.

Rummies — Nova Scotians who, in the late 19th and early 20th centuries, opposed the prohibition of alcohol.

Rum Runner — Smuggler of liquor during the era of prohibition also the person who goes to the liquor store to pick up the booze.

Runners — Sneakers.

Rutch — Fidget or restless; to move slowly.

~S~

Sally Ann — The Salvation Army.

Salt away — Stash or stow.

Same difference — Expression meaning that what is being stated is exactly the same as what you have already said.

Same old, same old — Nothing changes.

S'anyways — So anyway.

Scallop shucking — Open a scallop shell.

Scared the b'jesus out of me — Give you a fright.

Scarf it down — Eat very hurriedly.

Scoff — Eat quickly or a big meal.

Scarf it down

Scoff it off — Easily dismiss; shrug off.

Scooch — Move sideways.

Scotch cakes — A hearty oat cookie.

Scribbler — A notebook or a pad you write in.

Scrimey — Penny pinching, miserly.

Scrunchions — Fried cod tongues served in the Maritimes; can also be a term of endearment, especially when addressing young children.

Sea smoke — Heavy mist rising off the water when the air temperature suddenly becomes much colder than the ocean temperature.

Seen it, or, in some cases, "seen't" it — Saw it.

See you further on up the road — See you later.

See you when I see you — See you whenever.

Shedders — Soft-shelled lobster; can also be used to describe an animal that loses its fur.

She doesn't have her tongue in her pocket — She'll defend herself, verbally at least.

She's a hot one — Very hot day.

She's all gone — None left.

She's like a pig with a straw in its mouth — Woman who smokes.

She's never without an arse or an elbow — Always prepared.

She's running around like a blue-assed fly — Multitasking.

Shine the shit — Make something bad look good again.

Shinning — Working hard.

Shit a brick (shitting bricks) — Be afraid.

Shit before the shovel — Meant to be funny when letting someone else go first.

Shit disturber — Someone who willfully causes trouble.

Shit faced — Very drunk.

Shit fit — Loss of temper.

Shit for brains — Unintelligent.

Shit hawk — Seagull.

Shit in your blood — Always cold.

Shit-load — Large amount.

Shit on a stick — An angry exclamation.

Shit the bed — In a bad mood; screwed something up really badly.

Shit through the eye of a needle — Have diarrhea.

Shoot the fat — Have a conversation.

Variations:
Shoot the shit.

Shubenacadie Sam — Nova Scotia's own weather prognosticating rodent who lives in Shubenacadie Wildlife Park where he awaits his opportunity to strut his stuff on Groundhog Day, February 2. According to legend, if he sees his shadow and retreats to his burrow there will be six more weeks of winter but if he doesn't then there will be an early spring.

Shubenacadie Sam

Sideboards — Same as sideburns.

Side by each — Side by side.

Simmit — Woman's nightdress.

Six-pack — Half dozen of canned beer. (Even when they can come in eights, they're still called a six-pack.)

Skate — Untrustworthy; or to be slightly intoxicated.

Skid marks — Found in a boy's underwear, not on the road.

Skin flint — Very thrifty person.

Skinny as a rail — Very thin.

Variation:
Skinny as a rake handle.

Slack assed — Lazy.

Slack-jawed — Talks too much; tells too many lies.

Slammed — Very busy; over indulge.

Slap you silly — Hit.

Sleepers — Little pieces of dried, crusty fluid that gather in the corners of your eyes while you sleep.

Slicker than whale poop on ice — Untrustworthy.

Slimeball or slimebucket — Person with no socially redeeming values.

Slip a little lard onto it — Suggestion made when someone is trying to move something that won't budge.

Slipped a gear — Out of touch with current thinking.

Slipperier than snot — Extremely slippery.

Slippy — Slippery.

Smack-dab — Exact.

Smashed — Very intoxicated.

Smashers — Nova Scotians who, in the late 19th and early 20th centuries, desired a prohibition of alcohol.

Smarten up before I smack you upside the head — Stop acting like a fool.

Smells like winter — Signs of winter in the air.

Smelts — Small fish that are found in Nova Scotia rivers during the spring. For many, a feed of smelts is an annual tradition.

Smidge — Very small distance of measurement or a small amount.

Smooshed — Crushed.

SMU — (Pronounced smyou.) St. Mary's University.

Smudging — To cleanse or clear a place of evil spirits and to honour one's ancestors.

Smur — A foggy, dark haze on the horizon.

Snearly — Mean or hateful.

Snippy — Mean and short-tempered or superior feeling.

Snot locker — Nose.

Snow in the woodbox — Very bad off; no wood, only snow to burn.

Sobey's bags — All plastic bags regardless of which retail outlet they come from.

So cheap they could skin a louse (or flea) and tan the hide — Very stingy.

Sociable — A tradition in Nova Scotian bars; basically a toast.

Socked in — Very thick fog.

So didn't I — Me too; so did I.

So hungry I could eat a horse — Very hungry, famished.

Variations:
I'm so hungry I could eat the asshole out of a horse.
So hungry I could eat the asshole out of a skunk.

Solomon gundy — A common food in Nova Scotia made when salted herring is pickled in vinegar and spice.

Some — Very.

Some good — An exclamation of appreciation as in, "That supper was some good."

Variations:
Some awful good.
Right some good.

Something fierce — A lot, intensely.

Sook — Sulk.

South wind brings the rain — Belief that when the wind blows in from the south it means it's going to rain or when someone feels something bad will happen it usually does.

Sou'Wester — A waterproof hat worn by fishermen, usually yellow or black. Sometimes used to describe the person in a fun or conversely, insulting way.

Spit nails

Spilt — Spilled.

Spit nails — Very angry.

Spit through the eye of a needle — Cross.

Spleeny — Whiney or overly sensitive.

Spread the butter — To engage in intercourse.

Spritzing — Raining lightly.

> *Variation:*
> Spitting.

Square up — Settle a debt.

Squibbing — Hens clucking in the yard. Also, a gathering of women talking.

Steamed — Very angry.

Sternman — A lobsterman's helper (male or female) who does most of the pot hauling.

Steve — Name you call a man when you can't think of the guy's real name.

Sticky — Hot and humid weather.

Stitch in my side — Pain in side from overexertion.

Stogged up or stogged full — Full to the limit.

Stogg'er in — Fill it up any way you can.

Stop fressin' about things — Stop worrying.

> *Variation:*
> Stop fussin' about things.

Store bought — Something purchased as opposed to being made at home.

Stove up — Very busy.

Straight out — Going full tilt; being very busy.

Strawberrying — Picking strawberries.

Struck on his or herself — Conceited.

Strut around like a horny rooster in a hen house — Show off, try to impress.

Stuff it (where the sun don't shine) — Shove it up your rear.

Stump lifter — June bug.

Suck it up buttercup — Get over it!

Sugar wouldn't melt in his/her mouth — Everything always goes his/her way.

Variation:
Shit wouldn't melt in his/her mouth.

Sunshine — Not the obvious, but a term of endearment for someone you like.

Sunshine hours — Amount of hours of daylight.

Sunshower — A rain shower while the sun is out.

Sun will shine — Things will get better.

Suppa — Supper.

Stuck up — Snobbish.

Swampish — Sick to your stomach, nauseous.

Sweep it under the mat or rug — Hide the truth.

Variation: Sweep it out the back door.

Sweet dyin' Jesus — Expression of disbelief.

Swig — A small drink.

Take a bore down the road — Go for a drive.

Take a load off — Rest a spell.

Talk after him/her — Repeat what you heard; gossip.

Tanked — Stopped short as in "the car stopped without warning"; also, very drunk.

Tank trap — An area that is so muddy it could trap a tank.

Tarbish — A card game played primarily in Cape Breton.

Tastes after more — Delicious, think I'll have a second helping.

Tee-cha — Teacher.

Tend the house/kids — Mind the house; watch the children.

That ain't half bad — Pretty good.

That ain't nawthin' — No big deal.

That don't matter none — That doesn't matter at all.

That's all she wrote — It's over.

That's just nasty — Very bad.

That there — That one.

The backwoods — A place either within or outside of a town where people of lesser economic means may reside.

The bug — The flu or a cold.

The camp — A rustic building somewhere remote used a base for hunting and/or fishing.

Variation:
The cabin.

The City — What most people living outside of Halifax call Halifax.

The crud — A very bad cold.

The Fax — Halifax.

The fog is as thick as two quarts of shit in a one-quart bottle — Very thick fog.

The last twice — The last two times.

The LC — Liquor store.

The ocean is snotty — Rough sea.

The Old Man and/or The Old Woman — Dad or Mom; also husband or wife.

The Old People — People who came before us, ancestors.

There's a flight of stairs missing — Unintelligent.

The runs — Diarrhea.

Variation:
The trots.

The Valley — The Annapolis Valley.

The very best — Just great.

The whole shebang — Everything, total.

The Wife — Female spouse.

The wind's blowing sideways — To state the obvious.

The wind's going to be off — Starting to turn bad.

Them's fightin' words — The start of an argument.

Thick as pea soup — Very thick, foggy conditions.

Thick-o'-fog — Zero-visibility fog.

Variations:
'Tick 'o fog.
Thick of fog.

Thingamabob — Word substitute for a "word" you don't know or can't recall.

Thingamajig — Variation on thingamabob.

Thinks his/her shit don't stink — Conceited.

Three axe handles across the arse — Heavy.

Tidge — A very small distance of measurement.

Tight as lips on a woodpecker — Cheap, frugal.

Variation:
Tighter than a cow's ass at fly time.

Tighter than a frog's ass and that's watertight —
Very tight or close, as in close friends.

Time — A major party or celebration.

Time to dump this ice shack — Time to move to a
new house.

Titch — A measurement equal to a pinch or a drop.

Tizzy — Went crazy; flew into a rage.

To a Tee — Perfectly or completely.

To have a kink — Take a nap.

Tool — Someone incapable or unwilling to cooperate or
do anything.

Tongue lash — Yell at someone; to argue with someone.

Tongue wagger — Big talker.

Toot — Fart.

Tore a strip off — Got very mad at.

Toronto — Any place in Ontario.

Tough titty — Too bad, get over it.

Townie — Someone who lives in town.

TPBs — Trailer Park Boys.

Trucking right along — Moving forward at a steady pace.

Tuckered out — Very tired.

Turning the air blue — Cursing and swearing.

Turns my crank — Makes angry.

Turn the tides — Change things.

Twiddling away — Wasting time.

Twirly teet — Too early to eat.

Two clues short of a cart load — Unintelligent or confused.

Two-four — A case of 24 beer, usually cans.

Two-holer — Outside toilet with two holes.

Uglier than a can of smashed assholes — Very homely.

Ugly — Bad or foul mood.

Up against it — Hitting hard times.

Upalong — Beside the wharf or another vessel; also up along the river.

Up-chuck — Vomit or throw up.

Upland — Travel away from the ocean.

Variation:
Inland.

Up North — Toronto.

Upper Canada — Anywhere beyond New Brunswick.

Upper Canadian — Anyone who comes from someplace west of New Brunswick.

Up shore — Travel along the shore.

Up the stump — Pregnant.

Used me really good — Expression of gratefulness.

Useda — Used to.

Veronica — General name when you can't remember the real name.

Very best — Fine, thank you.

~W~

Warped — Odd, strange.

Washday — Laundry day, usually Monday.

Washington pie — A localized desert made with two thin white cakes held together with a layer of strawberry jam in the middle and covered in chocolate icing.

West Novas — Name of the West Nova Scotian Regiment that fought overseas in the Second World War.

Whack — A lot.

Whacked out or whacked in the head — Crazy or not with it.

What a caution he is — What a character.

What a dough head — Having little brain power.

What a piece of work — What a strange thing; a person who is difficult to deal with.

What a sin — Expression of empathy.

Whatever floats your boat — Make something suit your interest or need; if that's what makes you happy; to each their own.

Variations:
Whatever turns your crank.
Whatever blows your skirt up.
Whatever gets your oars wet.

Whatnot — Everything else.

What's his face — Used when you do not know or cannot recall a person's name.

Variations:
What's his name.
What's his nuts.

What's it — Thing.

What's up your arse? — What is the problem?

What's your father's name and where you from — Typical greeting between Nova Scotians who meet for the first time.

Whatyoumaycallit — Word used when you do not know or cannot remember the name of something.

When ducks quack — Likely, inevitable.

Whereabouts — Where?

Where's me boots — Time to get going; time to leave.

Where ya off to? — Where are you going?

Where y'at? — Where are you?

Variation:
Where you to?

Whirligig — A handcrafted toy that uses the wind to move its propellers.

Whizzed — Had a pee.

Whoopie pie — Chocolate cake-like snack that traditionally has a sweet, creamy, white filling. Can also be a term of endearment.

Who peed in your cornflakes? — Why are you cranky?

Well, who peed in your cornflakes?

Who'sit? — Who is it?

Wicked cold — Frigid.

Wicked good — Excellent.

Wind coming in — Storm approaching.

Wing-nut — Crazy.

Wired — Overly excited.

Wise-arse — Someone smart or witty.

Variation:
Wise-acker.

Wizzled — Wrinkled like a prune.

Woodsed her — Put a car off the road.

Woofed it down — Ate very fast.

Woof your cookies — Vomit or throw up.

Wouldn't say shit for a shovel full — Prim and proper.

Variation:
Wouldn't say shit for a mouthful.

Wound as tight as a hen's ass — Stressed out.

Wound up pretty good — Stressed out; ready for an argument or a fight.

X — A university in Antigonish (St. Francis Xavier.)

~Y~

Yeers yer car? — What year is your car?

Yer gonna drive me to drink — You are going to make me crazy.

Yer gonna drive me nuts (or crazy) — You are going to make me lose my sanity.

Yoke up — Hitch up a pair of oxen.

Yoked up

You — Hey, you!; also used to punctuate the end of sentence, as in 'That was right some good, you.'

You are something else — Don't really understand a person.

You'd shit yourself if you were well fed — You are not telling the truth; You are bragging.

You got a stick up your ass? — Are you in a bad mood?

You may as well wish in one hand and shit in the other; you'll get more out of it — It is futile or hopeless.

You old hen — You gossip.

Your ass is blowing wind — You are telling a lie.

You're all right; the world's all wrong — Back-handed compliment.

Your tongue can be tied in the middle and still wag on both ends — You talk a lot.

Your tongue can go like the clapper on a goose's ass — You talk quickly.

Youse — More than one you.

~Z~

Zip it — Stop talking.

Zonked — Very tired.

Zip it

Lobster jargon

Most jobs have a distinct language of their own. It describes local phenomena and events, outlines the history, and, more importantly, it binds people together in a bond of shared understanding.

Perhaps no other industry has more special verbage than the fishing industry and lobstering in particular, as these examples prove:

Berried — A female lobster laden with eggs.

Buoy — A floating, rounded, cork-shaped object usually made from Styrofoam that is tied with rope to mark where lobster traps are in the water. Fishermen paint their buoys a distinct colour scheme to differentiate themselves from the other fishermen.

Cock — A male lobster.

Crusher — The large lobster claw.

Cull — A lobster that is missing one of its front claws. They can usually be purchased for a bit cheaper.

Deckhand — The captain's helper who is responsible for emptying, baiting, and dropping traps, along with general boat clean up.

Gaff — A long, straight, wooden pole with a metal hook on the end used to hook the buoys attached to the lobster traps.

Hauler — An electronic device that is used to haul traps out of the water, located at the stern of the boat.

Hard shell — Hard shelled lobsters yield more than double the meat of soft-shelled or molting lobsters.

Hen — A female lobster.

Holding crates — The wooden crates that float just below the water's surface where lobsters are kept near shore until they go to market. Also called lobster cars.

Pistol — A lobster that has lost its two large claws, due to fighting with other lobsters or predators. Not to worry — these guys will eventually regenerate new ones.

Roe — Also known as "coral," this is a female lobster's egg sac. When raw, it is a bright orange-red colour, and when cooked, it turns coral pink. It is considered a delicacy, and is often added to sauces.

Sleeper — Be wary of these sluggish lobsters; they're so weak they cannot hold up their claws and are usually near death.

Soft shell — Lobsters molt their shell, and during this time it is best to avoid purchasing them as they result in less meat that's less flavourful.

Tinker — The little guys. The ones that have to be thrown back over board because they're too small.

Tomalley — Lobster liver. Some people love it, most people hate it; either way, it is prized for its taste and often added to sauces to boost flavour.

Tote — A plastic bin that lobster fishermen use to hold bait, lobster, and anything and everything on the boat that needs stowing. Also known as trays.

Trawl — A string of traps tied along a line; the line is marked by a buoy on each end.

V-notch — Used to mark breeding females, it is a small v-shaped cut in the lobster's flipper. If one of these is caught, it must be thrown back — whether carrying eggs or not.

16 x 22